Pinewood School Library
Los Altos, California

D0014711

WITHDRAWN

Texas

(Revised and Updated Edition)

by the Capstone Press
Geography Department

Content Consultant
Holly Taylor
Texas State Historical Association

CAPSTONE PRESS

MANKATO, MINNESOTA

C A P S T O N E   P R E S S

818 North Willow Street • Mankato, MN 56001
http://www.capstone-press.com

Copyright © 1996,1998 Capstone Press. All rights reserved. No part of this book may be reproduced without written permission from the publisher.

Printed in the United States of America.

Library of Congress Cataloging-in-Publication Data
Texas / Capstone Geography Department.
          p. cm. -- (One nation)
    Includes bibliographical references and index.
    Summary: Gives an overview of the state of Texas,
  including its history, geography, people, and living conditions.
    ISBN 1-56065-355-8
    1. Texas--Juvenile literature. [1. Texas.] I. Capstone
  Press Geography Dept. II. Series.
    F386.3.T36   1996
    976.4--dc20   95-49345
                                                        CIP
                                                        AC

Photo credits

International Stock Photos, cover.

Texas Department of Transportation, 4 (top), 5.

John Boykin, 30, 39, 42.

Archives Division, Texas State Library, 22, 26, 28.

Unicorn Stock/MacDonald Photography, 4 (bottom); Jeff Greenberg, 6, 15, 18;
   Mike Morris, 9; Les Van, 10; Dennis Thompson, 16, 30; H. Schmeiser, 21;
   Charles E. Schmidt, 25; Alice Prescott, 33; Jean Higgins, 34, 36.

Table of Contents

Fast Facts about Texas

State Flag

Location: In the southwestern United States
Area: 267,339 square miles (695,081 square kilometers)

Population: 16,986,510
Capital: Austin
Date admitted to the Union: December 29, 1845; the 28th state

Mockingbird

Bluebonnet

Largest cities: Houston, Dallas, San Antonio, El Paso, Austin, Fort Worth, Arlington, Corpus Christi, Lubbock, Garland
Nickname: The Lone Star State
State bird: Mockingbird
State flower: Bluebonnet

State tree: Pecan
State song: "Texas, Our Texas" by Gladys Yoakum Wright and William J. Marsh

Pecan tree

Chapter 1
Music in Texas

Country music is big in Texas. In fact, it is popular all over the country. Cowboys and cowgirls everywhere are putting on hats, boots, and jeans to dance to country hits.

They are doing line dances. They dance the cotton-eyed Joe. They swing to the Texas two-step. It all started in Texas and the South.

Country music has always been popular in Texas. Many famous country musicians were born there. Gene Autry, Clint Black, Waylon Jennings, George Jones, Willie Nelson, Buck

Dancing to country music is popular in Texas and throughout the United States.

Owens, George Strait, and Tanya Tucker are all from Texas. There are country-music radio stations throughout the state.

Texans like other kinds of music, too. Blues singers traveled from town to town in the early 20th century. They played at parties and at small clubs.

Some Texas jazz musicians used the blues sound. They put it in their own music. Texas rock and roll stars like Buddy Holly and Janis Joplin added the blues sound, too.

A Big Place

Texas is a big state. It was the largest state in the Union until Alaska became a state in 1959. Alaska is the only state bigger than Texas.

Texas has 305,951 miles (489,522 kilometers) of roads. This is the longest road system in the United States.

Texas was an independent nation before it became a state. It has been the home of three

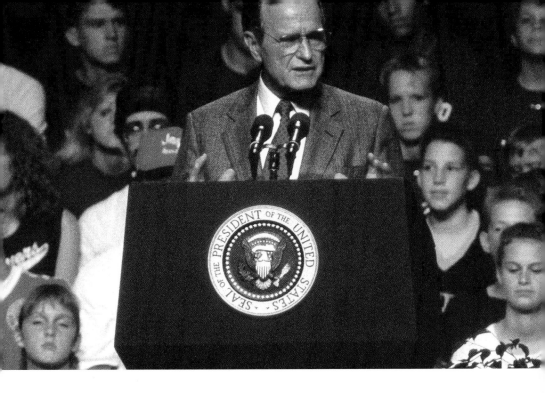

George Bush is one of three former U.S. presidents who have called Texas home.

U.S. presidents. They are Dwight Eisenhower, Lyndon Johnson, and George Bush.

Texans are proud of their state and its history. They call their state the Lone Star State. The name comes from the single star on the state flag.

Chapter 2

The Land

Because Texas is so big, it has many different types of land. Some of the land is forest. Some of it is mountains. Plains and deserts cover thousands of square miles.

West Texas

West Texas is hot and dry. Very little rain falls on the high plains, deserts, and mountains. There are few towns. Lonely roads stretch across the land. Rattlesnakes, coyotes, and bighorn sheep live in the region.

Deserts and mountains make up much of West Texas.

The Guadalupe Mountains are in West Texas. They are steep and rocky. Guadalupe Peak is near the border with New Mexico. It is 8,751 feet (2,625 meters) high. It is the highest point in Texas.

The Rio Grande forms the border between Texas and Mexico. The largest city in West Texas is El Paso. It is across the Rio Grande from the Mexican city of Juárez.

Central Texas

Plains spread across central and northern Texas. They take up more land than many U.S. states. Central Texas also includes the rocky Hill Country. The cities of Austin and San Antonio are in this part of Texas.

There are cattle ranches here, too. They have vast fields and pastures. Herds of longhorn cattle graze on the land.

The largest ranch in the United States is in north-central Texas. It is the Waggoner Ranch. It covers more than 800 square miles (2,080 square kilometers).

The Panhandle

Northwest Texas is called the Panhandle. The land is flat. There are few trees. Strong, cold winds blow there in the winter. Sometimes it snows. The Panhandle has thunderstorms and tornadoes in the spring and summer.

Amarillo is the largest city in the Panhandle. Palo Duro Canyon State Park is south of Amarillo. It has steep cliffs of layered rock.

East Texas

East Texas is covered with pine forests. The land is hilly. There are many small rivers. The fertile soil helps farmers grow rice, cotton, and vegetables.

The Sabine River forms the border with Louisiana. Across the Red River to the north is Oklahoma. The clay on the river bottom is a brownish-red color.

This is the rainiest part of the state. Summers in East Texas are hot, humid, and sometimes stormy. The major cities of East Texas include Tyler and Beaumont.

The Gulf Coast

Texas has a long coast on the Gulf of Mexico. The land is flat and sandy. Some alligators still live in the wetlands behind the Gulf beaches.

Padre Island is a long, narrow strip of sand.

Padre Island is a narrow strip of soft sand. It runs along the coast across from Corpus Christi. It goes south all the way to the Rio Grande and Mexico.

Hurricanes sometimes strike the Gulf Coast. A hurricane hit Galveston in 1900. There was no protection from the ocean waves. The storm killed more than 5,000 people. It was the worst natural disaster ever in the United States.

Chapter 3
The People

There are nearly 17 million people living in Texas. Only New York and California have more residents.

The strong Texas economy still attracts immigrants. About four percent of the state's population was born in a foreign country.

Europeans

About two-thirds of Texans have European roots. Many are descended from German, English, Irish, or Polish immigrants. These immigrants began arriving in the early 19th century.

Many people with German roots live in a town called New Braunfels. It is in central Texas, near

Nearly 17 million people live in Texas.

One out of every five Texans is Hispanic.

San Antonio.

Czech-speaking settlers moved into the surrounding plains. Texas also has many people with Scotch-Irish ancestors.

There are some small Cajun communities located in southeastern Texas. Cajuns are

French-speaking people. Their ancestors moved to the southern U.S. from Canada in the 18th century. Most Cajuns live in Louisiana.

Hispanic Americans

One out of every five Texans is Hispanic. South Texas has a large number of Hispanics. They speak Spanish or have Spanish-speaking ancestors.

Some Hispanics are descended from Mexican farmers. The farmers lived in Texas when it was a part of Mexico. San Antonio was founded by Mexicans in the early 18th century.

Every May 5th, Mexican Americans in Texas observe Cinco de Mayo. This holiday celebrates Hispanic culture with music, dancing, and food.

African Americans

African Americans make up about 12 percent of the population. Some of their ancestors were slaves who worked on plantations in Texas. Many former slaves became sharecroppers after the Civil War

(1861-1865). They paid rent for their homes with the crops they harvested. Some of the African-American men became cowboys on trail drives.

Many African Americans celebrate Juneteenth every year. It marks the day, June 19, 1865, that Texas slaves learned about the Emancipation Proclamation. President Abraham Lincoln issued the proclamation that freed the southern slaves on January 1, 1863, during the Civil War.

Asian Americans

Asian immigrants have come to Texas in recent times. They have come from Cambodia, Korea, and the Philippines.

Many Vietnamese people came to Texas in 1974 during the Vietnam War (1954-1975). Many of the Vietnamese immigrants worked as shrimpers in the Gulf of Mexico.

Native Americans

Texas has a small population of Native Americans. Most were forced to move

Texas has a small population of Native Americans.

out of the state in the 19th century. Many moved north to Oklahoma.

Texas has three reservations. The Kickapoo, Alabama-Coushatta, and Tigua Indians live on these lands. The reservations cover about 5,000 acres (2,000 hectares) of land.

Chapter 4

Texas History

Native Americans were the first people to live in Texas. Apache and Kiowa hunters lived in the mountains and on the plains. The Caddos included several different tribes. Tejas was a Caddo word meaning friend. Settlers turned the word Tejas into Texas.

Spanish Missions

The first European explorer to reach Texas was Alonso Álvarez de Piñeda. He sailed past

Stephen F. Austin helped build the first U.S. settlement in Texas. He brought 300 families with him.

the mouth of the Rio Grande in 1519. Spanish explorers claimed the land for Spain but did not settle there.

In 1682, Spanish priests built a mission at El Paso. Later, farmers from Mexico began settling north of the Rio Grande. They brought herds of cattle with them.

In 1685, an expedition of Frenchmen claimed Texas for France. René Robert Cavelier, Sieur de la Salle, led this group and tried to start a permanent French colony.

Spanish priests built more missions. Forts called presidios were built close to many of the missions. The presidios protected the missions from Indian attacks. A mission opened at San Antonio de Valero in 1718. Later, it was called the Alamo.

The Comanche and Kiowa Indians did not want people on their hunting grounds. They raided settlements and attacked missions. The raids drove many settlers out of Texas.

The Mexican army attacked the Alamo in February 1836.

Settlers from the United States arrived in 1821. Stephen F. Austin brought 300 families with him. They farmed along the Brazos River. That same year, Mexico won independence from Spain.

Revolt Against Mexico

Most Texans did not want to be a part of Mexico. A war broke out in 1835. The Mexican army was led by General Antonio López de Santa Anna. The army

The defenders of the Alamo fought to the death against the Mexican army. Mexico later lost the Texas Revolution.

attacked the Alamo in February 1836. Only 189 Texans were protecting the Alamo. Davy Crockett, Jim Bowie, and others fought to the death against more than 4,000 Mexican troops.

Texas fighters defeated the Mexican troops at the Battle of San Jacinto on April 21, 1836.

The Texans shouted "Remember the Alamo!" as they fought. Texas had won its independence from Mexico. It was now an independent country called the Republic of Texas. Sam Houston was the first elected president of the new republic.

Statehood

Texas became a state on December 29, 1845. The next year, war broke out between the United States and Mexico. The United States won the war in 1848. The Rio Grande became the border between Texas and Mexico.

Texas had been admitted to the Union as a slave state. The conflict over slavery and states' rights led to the Civil War in 1861. Texas and ten other southern states seceded from the Union. They formed the Confederacy.

In 1865, the South surrendered and the war ended. The last battle of the Civil War was at Palmito Ranch in Texas. It took place after the surrender. The news of the North's victory had not yet reached Texas. In 1870, Texas was readmitted to the Union.

Almost 50,000 barrels of oil spouted every day from an early gusher at Beaumont, Texas.

Cattle Drives and Oil Drilling

Many Texans established huge cattle ranches after the war. Cowboys drove the cattle north to markets in the Midwest.

The cattle drives ended in the 1880s. New railroads were built across the plains. Ranchers began moving their cattle by train.

The Texas economy changed in the 1890s. Wildcatters came to the state to drill for oil. The oil industry grew quickly.

War and Depression

The demand for oil was high during World War I (1914-1918). This drove up the price. Texas companies sold oil to the rest of the country.

The Great Depression (1929-1939) wrecked the nation's economy. The demand for oil dropped. Many oil workers lost their jobs. Many left for other states.

World War II (1939-1945) helped the Texas economy. New companies built ships, airplanes, and weapons for the war. Texas became an important manufacturing state.

From Texas to the Moon

Houston became the location of the Manned Spacecraft Center in the 1960s. Workers there directed the first mission to land on the moon in 1969.

Chapter 5

Texas Business

For many years, Texas depended on the oil industry. Today, Texas has many industries. This makes the state's economy one of the strongest in the nation.

Manufacturing

There are thousands of manufacturing companies in Texas. Chemical plants make rubber, plastic, and fertilizers. Food processing plants prepare vegetables, fish, and fruits. The food is shipped around the country.

Texas has become the home of many high-tech companies. High-tech companies make computers and electronic parts.

Oil drilling is still big business in Texas.

Agriculture

More cattle are raised in Texas than in any other state. Texas farmers also raise sheep, goats, and horses.

Farms in the Panhandle grow wheat, sorghum, and corn. Texas produces more than 4 million bales of cotton every year.

Fruit trees are common in the Rio Grande Valley. There are groves of grapefruit, orange, and nut trees.

Mining and Energy

Texas mines produce sulfur, coal, salt, and gypsum. Drilling teams search for underground oil and natural gas. Oil drilling is still a big business in Texas. Only four countries produce more oil than Texas.

Huge drilling platforms sit in the Gulf of Mexico. Pipelines carry the oil to refineries along the coast. These refineries turn the oil into gasoline.

More cattle are raised in Texas than in any other state.

Service Businesses

Seventy percent of Texas workers are
employed in service businesses. They work at
banks or insurance companies. They teach or
work in hospitals. They work in hotels or
restaurants or stores. Service businesses cover
many kinds of jobs.

Chapter 6
Seeing the Sights

Texas has many different landscapes. There are forests, canyons, seacoasts, and mountains to explore. Old forts and historic towns give visitors a look at the state's rich history.

There is something to do in every season. Rodeos and roundups are common in the fall. In the winter, bird lovers can watch thousands of migrating birds along the Gulf Coast. San Antonio holds a fiesta every spring. Water sports are popular on the lakes and rivers during the hot summers.

Visitors can see the sights of San Antonio by boat.

The boyhood home of Lyndon B. Johnson is near Johnson City.

West Texas

West Texas is the hottest part of Texas. It is also the most mountainous. Big Bend National Park is named for a sharp bend in the Rio Grande. Hiking trails in the park lead up mountains. The trails cross steep canyons. Visitors can spot bighorn sheep, wild deer, and antelope in the rocky hills.

The city of El Paso lies on the banks of the Rio Grande. Most of its residents are Hispanic. The Mexican city of Juárez is across the river. Fort Bliss is a huge military base north of El Paso.

Vast plains cover West Texas, too. Cattle and sheep graze on the ranges. Pumps bring oil up from the ground. Midland and Odessa are two important oil towns.

Central Texas

The Colorado River flows through central Texas. San Angelo and the capital of Austin are on the river. The Alamo still stands in downtown San Antonio. The city also has Riverwalk. This is an area of shops and restaurants along the San Antonio River.

The Lyndon Baines Johnson National Historical Park is near Johnson City. This was the home of the late President Lyndon Johnson.

East Texas

Much of East Texas is covered with pine forests. Dams on the rivers have created many artificial lakes. They are called reservoirs. One of these is Lake Texoma on the Red River. It is the largest lake in Texas.

Dallas and Fort Worth are two large cities in northeastern Texas. Every October, the Texas State Fair takes place in Dallas. It is the biggest state fair in the country. President John F. Kennedy was assassinated in Dallas on November 22, 1963. A museum and memorial plaza honor the president.

The Amon Carter Museum is in Fort Worth. The museum has a collection of western paintings and sculpture.

The Big Thicket Preserve is a dark, mysterious forest near the town of Kountze. Swamps and marshes surround the trees. Most people explore the Big Thicket in boats and canoes.

The Gulf Coast

Every winter, tourists from the northern U.S. visit the warm Gulf Coast. Padre Island National Seashore lies just off the coast. It is a long strip of sandy land. The island is 100 miles (160 kilometers) long.

Mission San Jose is in San Antonio. It is a reminder of the time Texas belonged to Spain and Mexico.

Corpus Christi is across from Padre Island. This is the deepest port on the Gulf. Across Corpus Christi Bay is Mustang Island. At one time, the island was home to a herd of wild horses.

Galveston is an important port. It lies on a small island in the Gulf. Old warehouses, commercial buildings, and homes there have been restored. A trolley called the Galveston

Flyer runs through town. Several fishing piers reach out into the Gulf.

Houston is the largest city in Texas. It has many skyscrapers and is the center of the oil industry.

The Johnson Space Center is just south of Houston. At Mission Control, visitors can watch engineers direct space flights. Moon rocks, space suits, and rockets are on display.

Texas Time Line

10,000 B.C.—The first people arrive in Texas.

A.D. 1400—The Caddo people are farming in Texas.

1519—Alonso Álvarez de Piñeda is the first European to explore Texas.

1682—Spanish mission is built near El Paso.

1685—René-Robert Cavelier, Sieur de La Salle, starts a colony on the Gulf Coast.

1718—The Alamo mission is founded.

1772—San Antonio becomes the center of Spanish government in Texas.

1821—Mexico wins its independence from Spain; Texas comes under Mexican control.

1836—Texas wins its independence from Mexico and sets up the Republic of Texas.

1845—Texas joins the Union as the 28th state.

1861—Texas leaves the Union and joins the Confederacy.

1866—Northbound cattle drives begin.

1870—Texas is readmitted to the Union.

1880s—Texas ranchers start using railroads to send cattle to market.

1894—Oil is found at Corsicana.

1918—Texas gives women the right to vote.

1925—Miriam "Ma" Ferguson becomes the first woman governor of Texas.

1930—The East Texas Oil Field is discovered.

1947—A ship explodes in the harbor of Texas City, killing 575 people.

1953—Texas-born Dwight D. Eisenhower becomes the 34th U.S. president.

1963—President John F. Kennedy is assassinated in Dallas; Lyndon B. Johnson, a Texan, becomes the 36th U.S. president.

1964—The Manned Spacecraft Center opens.

1989—George Bush from Houston becomes the 41st U.S. president.

1994, 1995—The Houston Rockets win the NBA Championship.

1995—Tejano singer Selena is murdered in Corpus Christi.

1996—The Dallas Cowboys win a fifth Super Bowl.

Famous Texans

Carol Burnett (1933-) Actress who hosted "The Carol Burnett Show" (1967-1978); born in San Antonio.

Henry Cisneros (1947-) Politician who became the first Hispanic-American mayor of a major U.S. city; born in San Antonio.

Dwight D. Eisenhower (1890-1969) Soldier and politician who served as the 34th U.S. president (1953-1961); born in Denison.

Lyndon Baines Johnson (1908-1973) Politician who served as the 36th president (1963-1969); born near Stonewall.

Barbara Jordan (1936-1996) First southern African-American woman elected to the U.S. House of Representatives (1973-1979); born in Houston.

Mary Martin (1913-1990) Actress known for her role as Peter Pan; born in Weatherford.

Willie Nelson (1933-) Singer and songwriter who created "outlaw" country music; born in Abbott.

Quanah Parker (1845?-1911) Comanche leader who encouraged his people to remember their heritage; born near Lubbock.

Selena Perez (1971-1995) Tejano singer whose album *Selena Live* won a Grammy Award (1994); born in Lake Jackson.

H. Ross Perot (1930-) Businessperson and politician who ran for U.S. president in 1992 and 1996; born in Texarkana.

Katherine Anne Porter (1890-1980) Novelist and short-story writer who won the Pulitzer Prize (1966); born in Indian Creek.

Ann Richards (1933-) Politician who served Texas as its second woman governor (1991-1995); born in Waco.

Nolan Ryan (1947-) Major league baseball pitcher who pitched seven no-hitters; born in Refugio.

Lee Trevino (1939-) Professional golfer who has won the U.S., British, and Canadian Opens all in one year (1971); born in Dallas.

Mildred "Babe" Didrikson Zaharias (1914-1956) Athlete who won two gold medals for track and field in the 1932 Olympics; born in Port Arthur.

Words to Know

ancestor—a person from whom one is descended, such as a grandmother or a great-grandfather

fertile—favorable to the growth of plants and crops

immigrant—a person who comes to another country to settle

jazz—improvised music originated by African Americans in the late 19th century

longhorn cattle—breed of cattle with long, spreading horns raised in the Southwest

natural disaster—destruction caused by natural events such as tornadoes, hurricanes, earthquakes, volcanoes, and blizzards

Panhandle—a strip of land in northwest Texas that looks like the handle of a pan

ranch—large farm in western North America on which cattle, horses, or sheep are raised

wildcatters—people who drill for oil in areas not known to have oil

To Learn More

Fradin, Dennis Brindell. *Texas.* From Sea to Shining Sea. Chicago: Children's Press, 1992.

Fritz, Jean. *Make Way for Sam Houston.* New York: Putnam, 1986.

Pelta, Kathy. *Texas.* Minneapolis: Lerner Publications, 1994.

Stein, R. Conrad. *Texas.* America the Beautiful. Chicago: Children's Press, 1989.

Internet Sites

City.Net Texas
http://www.city.net/countries/united_states/texas
Travel.org-Texas
http://www.travel.org/texas.html
State of Texas Government
http://info.texas.gov
Heart of Texas
http://hotx.com/hot/hotspots/nuhotindex.nclk

Useful Addresses

Johnson Space Center
2101 NASA Road 1
Houston, TX 77058

National Cowgirl Hall of Fame
515 Avenue B
Hereford, TX 79045

Sea World
10500 Sea World Drive
San Antonio, TX 78251

Texas Ranger Hall of Fame Museum
Box 2570
Waco, TX 76702

Index

████████████████████

███████████████████